YOUR AWKWARD

WORK

GETS

BETTER

a guided journal to
working better in
60 days

ANDY VARGO

Introduction

Work is a bummer, or at least it really can be. It doesn't have to stay that way. We all feel stuck at some point in our lives and the easiest thing to do is to just accept it and stay where we are. If we take the easy course, that is exactly how we will live the rest of our lives.

Perhaps you feel the only way to make work better is to find another job or restart your career. Well you may find that is the right course for you in the long run. However, if you do not first address the habits and attitude you bring to work every day, you will be stuck with more of the same no matter what career move you make. Even that dream job will get you down if you do not first focus on you.

Fear not, there is good news! You still have power over your life. Even if you are in a job you hate and find little pleasure in, you still have power.

All it takes is doing three simple things each day to bring your mind into focus. This journal will guide you, step by step, for sixty days, to help you develop better habits and a healthier mindset. Before you know it, you will be contributing to a healthier workplace. Who knows? You may even start to like it. And hey, if you decide to move on, you will be better equipped than ever to embark on a new adventure and get the most out of your change.

It's time to get started. Flip the page and learn how to create the changes you want to see in your own work life, one day at a time.

How To Use This Journal

So you are not happy with your career? What are you going to do about it? Each day will be the same as the last if you do nothing to make it better!

Going forward you are taking charge of your own fate. You control your workday and have the power to change where your career will take you!

It is very simple, a great day starts the night before. To set yourself up for a better work day, we are going to start before you go to bed.

Each day you will reflect on what you did that day to make the day better. Some days this may be very simple things. For example: I arrived ten minutes early, I stayed focused all day, or I took a healthy break. Try anything, no matter how simple.

Next, you will plan for tomorrow. This is a critical step, as you need to wake up knowing how you will take control of your career that day. This will leave no question what steps you will take to move your life in a more positive direction.

Each day I have written a focus point to help generate some thought. Do whatever you want and do not be afraid to repeat a focus as often as you need.

Now get productive creating the career you want!

Day One

Date: **Productivity Scale:**

Today I focused on these three things to make work better:

Did this: **Started the Work Gets Better Journal**

Didn't do this:

Learned or practiced this:

Tomorrow I will focus on these things to make work better:

Will do:

Won't do:

Will learn or practice learn:

Focus: Make a to-do list for your day. This will keep you on task throughout the day. Be sure to prioritize the most important tasks to be done first.

Some things to remember from today:

Something improved:

Something accomplished:

Something I am proud of:

Today's Word: **PRODUCTIVE**

Day Two

Date: **Productivity Scale:**

Today I focused on these three things to make work better:

Did this:

Didn't do this:

Learned or practiced this:

Tomorrow I will focus on these things to make work better:

Will do:

Won't do:

Will learn or practice:

Focus: Spend a day without gossip. See no gossip. Hear no gossip. Speak no gossip.

Some things to remember from today:

Something improved:

Something accomplished:

Something I am proud of:

Today's Word: **GROWTH**

Day Three

Date: **Productivity Scale:**

Today I focused on these three things to make work better:

Did this:

Didn't do this:

Learned or practiced this:

Tomorrow I will focus on these things to make work better:

Will do:

Won't do:

Will learn or practice:

Focus: Practice a skill that you have not used in the last six months.

Some things to remember from today:

Something improved:

Something accomplished:

Something I am proud of:

Today's Word: **SUCCESS**

Day Four

Date: **Productivity Scale:**

Today I focused on these three things to make work better:

Did this:

Didn't do this:

Learned or practiced this:

Tomorrow I will focus on these things to make work better:

Will do:

Won't do:

Will learn or practice:

Focus: Delegate at least two tasks today.

Some things to remember from today:

Something improved:

Something accomplished:

Something I am proud of:

Today's Word: **MENTOR**

Day Five

Date: **Productivity Scale:**

Today I focused on these three things to make work better:

Did this:

Didn't do this:

Learned or practiced this:

Tomorrow I will focus on these things to make work better:

Will do:

Won't do:

Will learn or practice:

Focus: No procrastinating today. Get those things crossed off your list sooner than later!

Some things to remember from today:

Something improved:

Something accomplished:

Something I am proud of:

Today's Word: **NETWORKING**

Day Six

Date: **Productivity Scale:**

Today I focused on these three things to make work better:

Did this:

Didn't do this:

Learned or practiced this:

Tomorrow I will focus on these things to make work better:

Will do:

Won't do:

Will learn or practice:

Focus: Learn a task that is not part of your responsibility. This will make you a more valuable and respected team member.

Some things to remember from today:

Something improved:

Something accomplished:

Something I am proud of:

Today's Word: **EXPERIENCE**

Day Seven

Date: **Productivity Scale:**

Today I focused on these three things to make work better:

Did this:

Didn't do this:

Learned or practiced this:

Tomorrow I will focus on these things to make work better:

Will do:

Won't do:

Will learn or practice:

Focus: Make a 'don't do' list. Write out those habits and distractions that pull you out of focus from your daily goals, and stay true to not doing them.

Some things to remember from today:

Something improved:

Something accomplished:

Something I am proud of:

Today's Word: **INFLUENCE**

Day Eight

Date: **Productivity Scale:**

Today I focused on these three things to make work better:

Did this:

Didn't do this:

Learned or practiced this:

Tomorrow I will focus on these things to make work better:

Will do:

Won't do:

Will learn or practice:

Focus: Don't allow negative thinking today! Pay attention to where your thoughts wander and when the thoughts are your inner bully, block them out.

Some things to remember from today:

Something improved:

Something accomplished:

Something I am proud of:

Today's Word: **LEADERSHIP**

Day Nine

Date: **Productivity Scale:**

Today I focused on these three things to make work better:

Did this:

Didn't do this:

Learned or practiced this:

Tomorrow I will focus on these things to make work better:

Will do:

Won't do:

Will learn or practice:

Focus: Learn something about the work history for two of your co-workers. Perhaps they have some hidden qualifications you did not know.

Some things to remember from today:

Something improved:

Something accomplished:

Something I am proud of:

Today's Word: **DELEGATE**

Day Ten

Date: **Productivity Scale:**

Today I focused on these three things to make work better:

Did this:

Didn't do this:

Learned or practiced this:

Tomorrow I will focus on these things to make work better:

Will do:

Won't do:

Will learn or practice:

Focus: Stand up for yourself, whether it's your boss, your coworker, or a subordinate, make sure you get credit for what you bring to the table.

Some things to remember from today:

Something improved:

Something accomplished:

Something I am proud of:

Today's Word: **INTEGRITY**

Day Eleven

Date: **Productivity Scale:**

Today I focused on these three things to make work better:

Did this:

Didn't do this:

Learned or practiced this:

Tomorrow I will focus on these things to make work better:

Will do:

Won't do:

Will learn or practice:

Focus: Schedule healthy and consistent breaks today!
Stepping away for just a few minutes will refresh your
perspective and renew your energy.

Some things to remember from today:

Something improved:

Something accomplished:

Something I am proud of:

Today's Word: **INSIGHT**

Day Twelve

Date: **Productivity Scale:**

Today I focused on these three things to make work better:

Did this:

Didn't do this:

Learned or practiced this:

Tomorrow I will focus on these things to make work better:

Will do:

Won't do:

Will learn or practice:

Focus: Clean and organize your work area before you start your day!

Some things to remember from today:

Something improved:

Something accomplished:

Something I am proud of:

Today's Word: **MOMENTUM**

Day Thirteen

Date: **Productivity Scale:**

Today I focused on these three things to make work better:

Did this:

Didn't do this:

Learned or practiced this:

Tomorrow I will focus on these things to make work better:

Will do:

Won't do:

Will learn or practice:

Focus: Don't hide your weaknesses today. Let people know where you could use help and which tasks aren't the best for you. This frees up time for you to use your strengths!

Some things to remember from today:

Something improved:

Something accomplished:

Something I am proud of:

Today's Word: **OWNERSHIP**

Day Fourteen

Date: **Productivity Scale:**

Today I focused on these three things to make work better:

Did this:

Didn't do this:

Learned or practiced this:

Tomorrow I will focus on these things to make work better:

Will do:

Won't do:

Will learn or practice:

Focus: Cooperate with others, even if you cannot see what's in it for you at the moment, be a team player.

Some things to remember from today:

Something improved:

Something accomplished:

Something I am proud of:

Today's Word: **RESOURCEFUL**

Day Fifteen

Date: **Productivity Scale:**

Today I focused on these three things to make work better:

Did this:

Didn't do this:

Learned or practiced this:

Tomorrow I will focus on these things to make work better:

Will do:

Won't do:

Will learn or practice:

Focus: Pack a healthy snack for the afternoon and be sure to take a break to eat it.

Some things to remember from today:

Something improved:

Something accomplished:

Something I am proud of:

Today's Word: **TEAM**

Day Sixteen

Date: **Productivity Scale:**

Today I focused on these three things to make work better:

Did this:

Didn't do this:

Learned or practiced this:

Tomorrow I will focus on these things to make work better:

Will do:

Won't do:

Will learn or practice:

Focus: Make a 'can-do' list. This is different from a to-do list, as it helps when you are overwhelmed to realistically focus on what you *can* get done.

Some things to remember from today:

Something improved:

Something accomplished:

Something I am proud of:

Today's Word: **INVENTIVE**

Day Seventeen

Date: **Productivity Scale:**

Today I focused on these three things to make work better:

Did this:

Didn't do this:

Learned or practiced this:

Tomorrow I will focus on these things to make work better:

Will do:

Won't do:

Will learn or practice:

Focus: Ask your boss for feedback. Maybe even go so far as to ask for a performance review.

Some things to remember from today:

Something improved:

Something accomplished:

Something I am proud of:

Today's Word: **DRIVE**

Day Eighteen

Date: **Productivity Scale:**

Today I focused on these three things to make work better:

Did this:

Didn't do this:

Learned or practiced this:

Tomorrow I will focus on these things to make work better:

Will do:

Won't do:

Will learn or practice:

Focus: Practice a skill that you hate to use. Don't worry about mastering it, just get a little more comfortable.

Some things to remember from today:

Something improved:

Something accomplished:

Something I am proud of:

Today's Word: **HONOR**

Day Nineteen

Date: **Productivity Scale:**

Today I focused on these three things to make work better:

Did this:

Didn't do this:

Learned or practiced this:

Tomorrow I will focus on these things to make work better:

Will do:

Won't do:

Will learn or practice:

Focus: Ask for help today on at least one project or task.

Some things to remember from today:

Something improved:

Something accomplished:

Something I am proud of:

Today's Word: **EFFORT**

Day Twenty

Date: **Productivity Scale:**

Today I focused on these three things to make work better:

Did this:

Didn't do this:

Learned or practiced this:

Tomorrow I will focus on these things to make work better:

Will do:

Won't do:

Will learn or practice:

Focus: Spend fifteen minutes creating a plan for being productive before you start your day.

Some things to remember from today:

Something improved:

Something accomplished:

Something I am proud of:

Today's Word: **RESPECT**

Day Twenty One

Date: **Productivity Scale:**

Today I focused on these three things to make work better:

Did this:

Didn't do this:

Learned or practiced this:

Tomorrow I will focus on these things to make work better:

Will do:

Won't do:

Will learn or practice:

Focus: Schedule times to read and respond to emails today and only check in at those times. Three times per day or every two hours works well.

Some things to remember from today:

Something improved:

Something accomplished:

Something I am proud of:

Today's Word: **VISION**

Day Twenty Two

Date: **Productivity Scale:**

Today I focused on these three things to make work better:

Did this:

Didn't do this:

Learned or practiced this:

Tomorrow I will focus on these things to make work better:

Will do:

Won't do:

Will learn or practice:

Focus: Mentor someone today. You will help someone learn
their job while learning even more yourself.

Some things to remember from today:

Something improved:

Something accomplished:

Something I am proud of:

Today's Word: **EVOLVE**

Day Twenty Three

Date: **Productivity Scale:**

Today I focused on these three things to make work better:

Did this:

Didn't do this:

Learned or practiced this:

Tomorrow I will focus on these things to make work better:

Will do:

Won't do:

Will learn or practice:

Focus: Don't let yourself be used today. Helping out can be great, but taking on too much will interfere with your own responsibilities.

Some things to remember from today:

Something improved:

Something accomplished:

Something I am proud of:

Today's Word: **COACH**

Day Twenty Four

Date: **Productivity Scale:**

Today I focused on these three things to make work better:

Did this:

Didn't do this:

Learned or practiced this:

Tomorrow I will focus on these things to make work better:

Will do:

Won't do:

Will learn or practice:

Focus: Start reading a book that will enhance your work experience. Time management, teamwork, or communications are all great topics.

Some things to remember from today:

Something improved:

Something accomplished:

Something I am proud of:

Today's Word: **CAPABLE**

Day Twenty Five

Date: **Productivity Scale:**

Today I focused on these three things to make work better:

Did this:

Didn't do this:

Learned or practiced this:

Tomorrow I will focus on these things to make work better:

Will do:

Won't do:

Will learn or practice:

Focus: Get in to work at least ten minutes early today. Take a few minutes to settle in and be ready to start your day out right.

Some things to remember from today:

Something improved:

Something accomplished:

Something I am proud of:

Today's Word: **TRAINING**

Day Twenty Six

Date: **Productivity Scale:**

Today I focused on these three things to make work better:

Did this:

Didn't do this:

Learned this or practiced:

Tomorrow I will focus on these things to make work better:

Will do:

Won't do:

Will learn or practice:

Focus: Listen to your favorite music on the way to work. Music affects your mood, and starting your day in a good mood will set you up for a great day!

Some things to remember from today:

Something improved:

Something accomplished:

Something I am proud of:

Today's Word: **TALENT**

Day Twenty Seven

Date: **Productivity Scale:**

Today I focused on these three things to make work better:

Did this:

Didn't do this:

Learned or practiced this:

Tomorrow I will focus on these things to make work better:

Will do:

Won't do:

Will learn or practice:

Focus: Ask a trusted peer for feedback on your performance. Others can see things we do not see in ourselves, the good and the bad.

Some things to remember from today:

Something improved:

Something accomplished:

Something I am proud of:

Today's Word: **GUIDANCE**

Day Twenty Eight

Date: **Productivity Scale:**

Today I focused on these three things to make work better:

Did this:

Didn't do this:

Learned or practiced this:

Tomorrow I will focus on these things to make work better:

Will do:

Won't do:

Will learn or practice:

Focus: Find a way to automate part of your day. Use an auto-responder, reorganize your inbox, or set scheduled times to meet with team members.

Some things to remember from today:

Something improved:

Something accomplished:

Something I am proud of:

Today's Word: **ENERGY**

Day Twenty Nine

Date: **Productivity Scale:**

Today I focused on these three things to make work better:

Did this:

Didn't do this:

Learned or practiced this:

Tomorrow I will focus on these things to make work better:

Will do:

Won't do:

Will learn or practice:

Focus: Don't eat at your desk today. It may seem productive to 'push through' and grab a quick bite, but the reality is you are robbing yourself the chance to properly recharge.

Some things to remember from today:

Something improved:

Something accomplished:

Something I am proud of:

Today's Word: **CHALLENGE**

Day Thirty

Date: **Productivity Scale:**

Today I focused on these three things to make work better:

Did this:

Didn't do this:

Learned or practiced this:

Tomorrow I will focus on these things to make work better:

Will do:

Won't do:

Will learn or practice:

Focus: Write out the business plan of you. Where will you take yourself in the next year? How will you get there?

Some things to remember from today:

Something improved:

Something accomplished:

Something I am proud of:

Today's Word: **TRUTH**

Day Thirty One

Date: **Productivity Scale:**

Today I focused on these three things to make work better:

Did this:

Didn't do this:

Learned or practiced this:

Tomorrow I will focus on these things to make work better:

Will do:

Won't do:

Will learn or practice:

Focus: Use the right safety gear for your job. Whether it's goggles, a vest, or an ergonomic keyboard and mouse.

Some things to remember from today:

Something improved:

Something accomplished:

Something I am proud of:

Today's Word: **TRIUMPH**

Day Thirty Two

Date: **Productivity Scale:**

Today I focused on these three things to make work better:

Did this:

Didn't do this:

Learned or practiced this:

Tomorrow I will focus on these things to make work better:

Will do:

Won't do:

Will learn or practice:

Focus: Don't start any new projects today until you have
completed at least on that is already on your list.

Some things to remember from today:

Something improved:

Something accomplished:

Something I am proud of:

Today's Word: **DIRECTION**

Day Thirty Three

Date: **Productivity Scale:**

Today I focused on these three things to make work better:

Did this:

Didn't do this:

Learned or practiced this:

Tomorrow I will focus on these things to make work better:

Will do:

Won't do:

Will learn or practice:

Focus: Learn one aspect of your boss's job. This will make you more valuable while giving you a better perspective of the bigger picture.

Some things to remember from today:

Something improved:

Something accomplished:

Something I am proud of:

Today's Word: **INSPIRE**

Day Thirty Four

Date: **Productivity Scale:**

Today I focused on these three things to make work better:

Did this:

Didn't do this:

Learned or practiced this:

Tomorrow I will focus on these things to make work better:

Will do:

Won't do:

Will learn or practice:

Focus: Grow your network in person. Attend a networking
event or work conference and be sure to bring your cards!

Some things to remember from today:

Something improved:

Something accomplished:

Something I am proud of:

Today's Word: **ENCOURAGE**

Day Thirty Five

Date: Productivity Scale:

Today I focused on these three things to make work better:

Did this:

Didn't do this:

Learned or practiced this:

Tomorrow I will focus on these things to make work better:

Will do:

Won't do:

Will learn or practice:

Focus: Do your least favorite task before you do anything else today!

Some things to remember from today:

Something improved:

Something accomplished:

Something I am proud of:

Today's Word: **KNOWLEDGE**

Day Thirty Six

Date: **Productivity Scale:**

Today I focused on these three things to make work better:

Did this:

Didn't do this:

Learned or practiced this:

Tomorrow I will focus on these things to make work better:

Will do:

Won't do:

Will learn or practice:

Focus: Shop the competition. Whether it's another company, or someone you are competing against for a promotion, find out what they are doing right.

Some things to remember from today:

Something improved:

Something accomplished:

Something I am proud of:

Today's Word: **TEAMWORK**

Day Thirty Seven

Date: **Productivity Scale:**

Today I focused on these three things to make work better:

Did this:

Didn't do this:

Learned or practiced this:

Tomorrow I will focus on these things to make work better:

Will do:

Won't do:

Will learn or practice:

Focus: Update your resume. Even if you are happy where you are, it will empower you to understand your experience.

Some things to remember from today:

Something improved:

Something accomplished:

Something I am proud of:

Today's Word: **INTUITION**

Day Thirty Eight

Date: **Productivity Scale:**

Today I focused on these three things to make work better:

Did this:

Didn't do this:

Learned or practiced this:

Tomorrow I will focus on these things to make work better:

Will do:

Won't do:

Will learn or practice:

Focus: Do not allow bad self-talk today.

Some things to remember from today:

Something improved:

Something accomplished:

Something I am proud of:

Today's Word: **POWER**

Day Thirty Nine

Date: **Productivity Scale:**

Today I focused on these three things to make work better:

Did this:

Didn't do this:

Learned or practiced this:

Tomorrow I will focus on these things to make work better:

Will do:

Won't do:

Will learn or practice:

Focus: Watch a tutorial video today. Pick a topic you want to improve and search it online.

Some things to remember from today:

Something improved:

Something accomplished:

Something I am proud of:

Today's Word: **INTERACT**

Day Forty

Date: **Productivity Scale:**

Today I focused on these three things to make work better:

Did this:

Didn't do this:

Learned or practiced this:

Tomorrow I will focus on these things to make work better:

Will do:

Won't do:

Will learn or practice:

Focus: Practice clear communication today. Through email, conversations, and texts, be sure your message is clear.

Some things to remember from today:

Something improved:

Something accomplished:

Something I am proud of:

Today's Word: **DISCERN**

Day Forty One

Date: **Productivity Scale:**

Today I focused on these three things to make work better:

Did this:

Didn't do this:

Learned or practiced this:

Tomorrow I will focus on these things to make work better:

Will do:

Won't do:

Will learn or practice:

Focus: Mix up your routine. If you normally eat in the cafeteria, try getting out of the building. Flip things around and see if it stirs up any new perspectives and ideas.

Some things to remember from today:

Something improved:

Something accomplished:

Something I am proud of:

Today's Word: **SKILL**

Day Forty Two

Date: **Productivity Scale:**

Today I focused on these three things to make work better:

Did this:

Didn't do this:

Learned or practiced this:

Tomorrow I will focus on these things to make work better:

Will do:

Won't do:

Will learn or practice:

Focus: Practice public speaking. Whether training a group in the conference room, or telling a story in the breakroom, get up in front of people and talk.

Some things to remember from today:

Something improved:

Something accomplished:

Something I am proud of:

Today's Word: **IMPACT**

Day Forty Three

Date: **Productivity Scale:**

Today I focused on these three things to make work better:

Did this:

Didn't do this:

Learned or practiced this:

Tomorrow I will focus on these things to make work better:

Will do:

Won't do:

Will learn or practice:

Focus: Start tomorrow out right by going to bed early tonight. Give your mind time to wind down before you fall to sleep.

Some things to remember from today:

Something improved:

Something accomplished:

Something I am proud of:

Today's Word: **EXERCISE**

Day Forty Four

Date: **Productivity Scale:**

Today I focused on these three things to make work better:

Did this:

Didn't do this:

Learned or practiced this:

Tomorrow I will focus on these things to make work better:

Will do:

Won't do:

Will learn or practice:

Focus: Spend the last fifteen minutes of your day cleaning up and preparing an organized work area for tomorrow so you can start your day out right.

Some things to remember from today:

Something improved:

Something accomplished:

Something I am proud of:

Today's Word: **CHARACTER**

Day Forty Five

Date: **Productivity Scale:**

Today I focused on these three things to make work better:

Did this:

Didn't do this:

Learned or practiced this:

Tomorrow I will focus on these things to make work better:

Will do:

Won't do:

Will learn or practice:

Focus: Get a study buddy! Find a colleague who also wants to improve their skill level and practice new things together. Perhaps you can tutor each other from your own strengths.

Some things to remember from today:

Something improved:

Something accomplished:

Something I am proud of:

Today's Word: **ACCOUNTABILITY**

Day Forty Six

Date: **Productivity Scale:**

Today I focused on these three things to make work better:

Did this:

Didn't do this:

Learned or practiced this:

Tomorrow I will focus on these things to make work better:

Will do:

Won't do:

Will learn or practice:

Focus: Use your lunch time to put good vibes into your day.
Watch funny videos online, read the next chapter of a book,
or call a friend to say hi.

Some things to remember from today:

Something improved:

Something accomplished:

Something I am proud of:

Today's Word: **COLLABORATE**

Day Forty Seven

Date: **Productivity Scale:**

Today I focused on these three things to make work better:

Did this:

Didn't do this:

Learned or practiced this:

Tomorrow I will focus on these things to make work better:

Will do:

Won't do:

Will learn or practice:

Focus: Create a list of accomplishments for this year. Start with the beginning of the year, or your last performance review, and add in the things you are most proud of.

Some things to remember from today:

Something improved:

Something accomplished:

Something I am proud of:

Today's Word: **ACUMEN**

Day Forty Eight

Date: **Productivity Scale:**

Today I focused on these three things to make work better:

Did this:

Didn't do this:

Learned or practiced this:

Tomorrow I will focus on these things to make work better:

Will do:

Won't do:

Will learn or practice:

Focus: Get to know team members you may not. Make friends with the janitor, security, or front desk personnel. Show them you appreciate them and it may come in handy.

Some things to remember from today:

Something improved:

Something accomplished:

Something I am proud of:

Today's Word: **RELIABILITY**

Day Forty Nine

Date: **Productivity Scale:**

Today I focused on these three things to make work better:

Did this:

Didn't do this:

Learned or practiced this:

Tomorrow I will focus on these things to make work better:

Will do:

Won't do:

Will learn or practice:

Focus: Plan distraction free work time. Lock yourself in a room, put in headphones, whatever you have to do to be alone and stay focused for 90 minutes of work time.

Some things to remember from today:

Something improved:

Something accomplished:

Something I am proud of:

Today's Word: **PREPARE**

Day Fifty

Date: **Productivity Scale:**

Today I focused on these three things to make work better:

Did this:

Didn't do this:

Learned or practiced this:

Tomorrow I will focus on these things to make work better:

Will do:

Won't do:

Will learn or practice:

Focus: Drink plenty or water all day. You should be refilling your water glass several times and going to the restroom. Annoying but healthy! Hydration will help you focus better.

Some things to remember from today:

Something improved:

Something accomplished:

Something I am proud of:

Today's Word: **WISDOM**

Day Fifty One

Date: **Productivity Scale:**

Today I focused on these three things to make work better:

Did this:

Didn't do this:

Learned or practiced this:

Tomorrow I will focus on these things to make work better:

Will do:

Won't do:

Will learn or practice:

Focus: Do something to make work fun today! Tell a joke, play a game, or share stories in the breakroom. When work is more fun, everyone will relax and work better.

Some things to remember from today:

Something improved:

Something accomplished:

Something I am proud of:

Today's Word: **PROSPER**

Day Fifty Two

Date: **Productivity Scale:**

Today I focused on these three things to make work better:

Did this:

Didn't do this:

Learned or practiced this:

Tomorrow I will focus on these things to make work better:

Will do:

Won't do:

Will learn or practice:

Focus: List the pain points at work with your ideas for the best solutions. Valuable team members bring solutions to their leaders, not problems.

Some things to remember from today:

Something improved:

Something accomplished:

Something I am proud of:

Today's Word: **CONFIDENCE**

Day Fifty Three

Date: **Productivity Scale:**

Today I focused on these three things to make work better:

Did this:

Didn't do this:

Learned or practiced this:

Tomorrow I will focus on these things to make work better:

Will do:

Won't do:

Will learn or practice:

Focus: Have coffee with a colleague. One rule, no gossip.
Just get to know each other and learn from your experiences.

Some things to remember from today:

Something improved:

Something accomplished:

Something I am proud of:

Today's Word: **ENGAGE**

Day Fifty Four

Date: **Productivity Scale:**

Today I focused on these three things to make work better:

Did this:

Didn't do this:

Learned or practiced this:

Tomorrow I will focus on these things to make work better:

Will do:

Won't do:

Will learn or practice:

Focus: List out your top five skills and talents. Give yourself credit for all of the work you have done to get to where you are today. Keep this handy for your down days.

Some things to remember from today:

Something improved:

Something accomplished:

Something I am proud of:

Today's Word: **IMPLEMENT**

Day Fifty Five

Date: **Productivity Scale:**

Today I focused on these three things to make work better:

Did this:

Didn't do this:

Learned or practiced this:

Tomorrow I will focus on these things to make work better:

Will do:

Won't do:

Will learn or practice:

Focus: Do any task that requires less than five minutes to complete as it comes your way. Cross them off before they ever make it onto a list.

Some things to remember from today:

Something improved:

Something accomplished:

Something I am proud of:

Today's Word: **BALANCE**

Day Fifty Six

Date: **Productivity Scale:**

Today I focused on these three things to make work better:

Did this:

Didn't do this:

Learned or practiced this:

Tomorrow I will focus on these things to make work better:

Will do:

Won't do:

Will learn or practice:

Focus: Eat a healthy breakfast. They say it is the most important meal of the day, but how often do you skip it altogether?

Some things to remember from today:

Something improved:

Something accomplished:

Something I am proud of:

Today's Word: **STUDY**

Day Fifty Seven

Date: **Productivity Scale:**

Today I focused on these three things to make work better:

Did this:

Didn't do this:

Learned or practiced this:

Tomorrow I will focus on these things to make work better:

Will do:

Won't do:

Will learn or practice:

Focus: Take a few minutes to watch a motivational video.
You may get a new perspective, rush of energy, or even just a
quick tip to cope with an overwhelming day.

Some things to remember from today:

Something improved:

Something accomplished:

Something I am proud of:

Today's Word: **ACHIEVE**

Day Fifty Eight

Date: **Productivity Scale:**

Today I focused on these three things to make work better:

Did this:

Didn't do this:

Learned or practiced this:

Tomorrow I will focus on these things to make work better:

Will do:

Won't do:

Will learn or practice:

Focus: Go outside during your lunch break. Fresh air will renew your senses and set you up for a great start to the afternoon.

Some things to remember from today:

Something improved:

Something accomplished:

Something I am proud of:

Today's Word: **AWARE**

Day Fifty Nine

Date: **Productivity Scale:**

Today I focused on these three things to make work better:

Did this:

Didn't do this:

Learned or practiced this:

Tomorrow I will focus on these things to make work better:

Will do:

Won't do:

Will learn or practice:

Focus: Asses your improvement from day one. Be honest about your productivity and stress level during your work day. Make notes on areas you would like to focus on next.

Some things to remember from today:

Something improved:

Something accomplished:

Something I am proud of:

Today's Word: **PARTICIPATE**

Day Sixty

Date: **Productivity Scale:**

Today I focused on these three things to make work better:

Did this:

Didn't do this:

Learned or practiced this:

Tomorrow I will focus on these things to make work better:

Will do:

Won't do:

Will learn or practice:

Focus: Celebrate! You made it through sixty days of gradual improvement. Celebrate with a long lunch and treat yourself to dessert!

Some things to remember from today:

Something improved:

Something accomplished:

Something I am proud of:

Today's Word: **PROGRESS**

Conclusion

You did it! You made it through two months of improving your work day, step by step, one day at a time. How do you feel?

My hope is that you feel confident, productive, and in control of your career. I hope that you have created new habits and learned new skills that will take you wherever you want to go. I hope that you feel that you have the power to steer your career in the direction you want.

What's next?

It's simple, keep going. Keep developing new habits and learning new skills every day. Keep finding ways to network and mentor others at work. Continue to use the power you have to create your best situation.

If you need to, start a new journal filled with more focus points. Look back through these pages and highlight your greatest achievements. Find the things that made the biggest impact on you, and recreate those practices.

Share.

Share with your friends. Share with your colleagues. Share with those who may need some help with the feeling that work will always be just a bummer. Show them the power they already have to control their career.

After all, this is not the end. This is just...

The Start

About the Author

Do you feel like you are always two steps away from your big break? Then you can understand how Andy Vargo lived the first forty years of his life. Coming out of the closet at forty doesn't define him, pursuing his passion to help others does. Andy works corporate and school events as a motivational speaker and helps people live their fullest lives as a one on one life coach. At night you can find him working stages around the northwest as a comedian making light of his journey with the gift of laughter. Awkward is not only his brand, but his style as Andy encourages us all to 'Own Our Awkward' and be true to our genuine selves.

Andy hosts the podcast, *Own Your Awkward*, and shares thoughts and ideas in his blog and video series available at awkwardcareer.com.

Continue Your Journey

Need help pulling yourself up?

Order the first book in the *Awkward Journal* series:
Your Awkward Life Gets Better.

Now Available

Is your life boring?

Order the second book in the *Awkward Journal* series,
Your Awkward Life Gets Funner.

Now Available

Need help accepting yourself?

Order the fourth book in the *Awkward Journal* series:
Your Awkward Life Gets Gayer.

Now Available